Do You Really Want a Turtle?

Bridget Heos • Illustrated by Katya Longhi

Amicus Illustrated is published by Amicus
P.O. Box 1329, Mankato, MN 56002
www.amicuspublishing.us

Library of Congress Cataloging-in-Publication Data
Heos, Bridget, author.
 Do you really want a turtle? / by Bridget Heos ; illustrated by Katya Longhi.
    pages cm. — (Amicus illustrated) (Do you really want a pet?)
 Summary: "Several turtles (and the narrator) teach a young girl the
responsibility—and the joys—of caring for a pet turtle. Includes "Is this pet
right for me?" quiz— Provided by publisher.
 Audience: K to grade 3.
 Includes bibliographical references.
 ISBN 978-1-60753-752-6 (library binding) — ISBN 978-1-60753-851-6 (ebook)
1. Turtles as pets—Juvenile literature. 2. Pets—Juvenile literature. I. Longhi, Katya,
illustrator. II. Title. III. Series: Heos, Bridget. Do you really want a pet?
SF459.T8H46 2015
639.3'92—dc23   2014033271

Editor   Rebecca Glaser
Designer   Kathleen Petelinsek

Printed in the United States of America

10 9 8 7 6 5 4 3 2

About the Author

Bridget Heos is the author of more than
70 books for children including *Mustache Baby*
and *Mustache Baby Meets His Match*. Her family
has two pets, an old dog named Ben and a young
cat named Homer. You can find out more about
her at www.authorbridgetheos.com.

About the Illustrator

Katya Longhi was born in southern Italy.
She studied illustration at the Nemo NT
Academy of Digital Arts in Florence. She loves
to create dream worlds with horses, flying
dogs, and princesses in her illustrations.
She currently lives in northern Italy
with her Prince Charming.

So you say you want a turtle. You really want a turtle.

But do you really want a turtle?

Or do you want a tortoise?

Turtles and tortoises are related. Most turtles spend more time in water than tortoises do. Box turtles spend much of their time on land.

RED-EARED SLIDER TURTLE

BOX TURTLE

PAINTED TURTLE

All turtles and tortoises live long lives.
Box turtles can reach the ripe old age of 100!

Are you ready to grow old together?

Okay, then you'll need a home for your turtle. Box turtles and tortoises like sunshine and fresh air.

In the summertime, an outside home is best.

Build a pen in your yard. Make sure your pet can't dig or crawl out. There should be plenty of room for exercising, a small bath to swim in, and a hideout for sleeping.

Slow and steady wins the race!

You can even plant your turtle a garden...

. . . of grass and weeds! Box turtles and tortoises love eating dandelions.

Always stop to eat the flowers!

Box turtles also eat animals. You can feed them insects, slugs, and earthworms. And don't forget dessert! Both box turtles and tortoises will eat fruits and berries as a treat.

In the fall, you can help your box turtle or tortoise hibernate. You can put your pet in a box filled with leaves. Turtles need moisture when they hibernate. Tortoises do not.

Aww, come on! One more story?

Set the box in your basement or garage. (Make sure it doesn't freeze!) Check on your turtle every week. In the spring, bring your turtle back outside.

Your turtle probably didn't miss you. Box turtles and tortoises don't need hugs. They don't like being picked up. But you can rub the backs of their heads! Just wash your hands afterwards. All reptiles have bacteria on their skin.

What if you choose a water turtle? Water turtles are kept in aquariums. Fill the aquarium halfway with water. Add rocks for the turtle to climb onto. Because after all that swimming . . .

. . . it needs a break! In nature, turtles like to bask in the sun. So you'll need a fluorescent light and heat lamp to mimic the sun.

Water turtles eat both meat and plants. They eat earthworms, insects, and guppies. As they grow, they eat more plants and vegetables. And they poop a lot!

A water filter will help. But you'll still need to clean the aquarium. First, take out your turtle and put it in a container filled with water.

Empty the aquarium. Scrub it, along with the rocks. Then put in clean water and put the rocks back.

Now your turtle can come back home. Wash your hands!

Turtles and tortoises aren't the touchy-feely type. But they are cool pets. Did you know they have been alive since the Age of Dinosaurs?

What's up, T-rex?

So if you're willing to feed, water, and provide a good habitat for your pet, then maybe you really do want a turtle or tortoise.

Now I have a question for the turtle. You say you want a person. You really, really want a person.

But do you *really* want a person?

QUIZ

Is this the right pet for me?

Should you get a turtle or tortoise? Complete this quiz to find out. (Be sure to talk to breeders, rescue groups, or pet store workers, too!)

1. Can you care for a turtle for 30, 40, or 50 years, or even longer?
2. Do you have space for an outdoor pen?
3. Would you like having a pet that lives in an aquarium?
4. Are you okay with not cuddling with your pet?

If you answered . . .

a. NO TO ONE, consider a shorter-lived pet, like a lizard.
b. NO TO TWO, you might want a water turtle instead of a box turtle or tortoise.
c. NO TO THREE, a box turtle or tortoise might be better.
d. NO TO FOUR, choose an animal that likes to cuddle, like a dog, cat, rabbit, or guinea pig.
e. YES TO 1 AND 4, AND either 2 or 3, then a turtle or tortoise might be the right pet for you!

Websites

Austin's Turtle Page
www.austinsturtlepage.com
This site is written by a person who has owned many turtles. See photos of pet turtles, talk with other turtle owners, and read articles about different species of turtles and tortoises.

California Turtle and Tortoise Club
tortoise.org
This group has information and resources about caring for pet turtles.

How to Care for Your Box Turtle
www.wikihow.com/Care-for-Your-Box-Turtle
Step-by-step instructions for what you will need to do if you get a box turtle.

Reptiles Magazine
www.reptilesmagazine.com
Reptiles Magazine offers articles about reptiles and pet care information.

Every effort has been made to ensure that these websites are appropriate for children. However, because of the nature of the Internet, it is impossible to guarantee that these sites will remain active indefinitely or that their contents will not be altered.

Read More

Carraway, Rose. *Terrific Turtles*. New York: Gareth Stevens, 2012.

Hamilton, Lynn. *My Pet Turtle*. New York: Weigl, 2010.

Sexton, Colleen. *Caring for Your Turtle*. Minneapolis: Bellwether Media, 2011.

Stevens, Kathryn. *Turtles*. Mankato, Minn.: The Child's World, 2009.

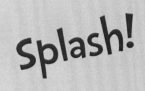

Splash!